WHAT ARE THE 7 WONDERS OF THE MODERN WORLD?

Doreen Gonzales

Enslow Publishers, Inc.
40 Industrial Road
Box 398
Berkeley Heights, NJ 07922
USA

http://www.enslow.com

Original edition published as *Seven Wonders of the Modern World* in 2005.

Library of Congress Cataloging-in-Publication Data

Gonzales, Doreen.
    What are the 7 wonders of the modern world? / Doreen Gonzales.
       p. cm.
    Includes bibliographical references and index.
    Summary: "Learn about the Seven Wonders of the Modern World: The Panama Canal, North Sea Protection Works, the Empire State Building, the Golden Gate Bridge, The Burj Khalifa, The Itaipu Dam, and the Channel Tunnel"—Provided by publisher.
    ISBN 978-0-7660-4152-3
    1. Seven Wonders of the World—Juvenile literature. 2. Engineering—Juvenile literature. 3. Architecture—Juvenile literature. 4. Buildings—Juvenile literature. I. Title. II. Title: What are the seven wonders of the modern world?
    TA149.G644 2012
    624—dc23

2012009141

Future editions:
Paperback ISBN: 978-1-4644-0231-9
Single-User PDF ISBN: 978-1-4646-1150-6
EPUB ISBN: 978-1-4645-1151-6
Multi-User PDF ISBN: 978-0-7660-5779-1

Printed in the United States of America.

112012 Lake Book Manufacturing, Inc., Melrose Park, IL

10 9 8 7 6 5 4 3 2 1

To Our Readers: We have done our best to make sure all Internet addresses in this book were active and appropriate when we went to press. However, the author and the publisher have no control over and assume no liability for the material available on those Internet sites or on other Web sites they may link to. Any comments or suggestions can be sent by e-mail to comments@enslow.com or to the address on the back cover.

♻ Enslow Publishers, Inc., is committed to printing our books on recycled paper. The paper in every book contains 10% to 30% post-consumer waste (PCW). The cover board on the outside of each book contains 100% PCW. Our goal is to do our part to help young people and the environment too!

Photo Credits: © 1999 PhotoDisc, p. 8; Angelo Arcadi/© 2011 Photos.com, a division of Getty Images. All rights reserved., p. 31; AP Images, Str, p. 41; Charles Lytton/© 2011 Photos.com, a division of Getty Images. All rights reserved., p. 10; © Enslow Publishers, Inc., p. 7; © iStockphoto.com/clubfoto, p. 38; Iladm/© 2012 Photos.com, a division of Getty Images. All rights reserved., p. 36; Jose Gil/© 2011 Photos.com, a division of Getty Images. All rights reserved., p. 20; Juho Ruohola/© 2012 Photos.com, a division of Getty Images. All rights reserved., p. 29; jvfdwolf/© 2011 Photos.com, a division of Getty Images. All rights reserved., p. 17; Nancy Nehring/© 2011 Photos.com, a division of Getty Images. All rights reserved., p. 12; Rahhal/Shutterstock.com, p. 31; © 2011 Photos.com, a division of Getty Images. All rights reserved., pp. 1, 4, 25, 34; Shutterstock.com, pp. 15, 23, 31, 36.

Cover Photo: From top: AP Images, Str (The Channel Tunnel); © 2011 Photos.com, a division of Getty Images. All rights reserved. (The Golden Gate Bridge); Juho Ruohola/© 2012 Photos.com, a division of Getty Images. All rights reserved. (Burj Khalifa); Shutterstock.com (The Itaipu Dam); © 1999 PhotoDisc, (The Empire State Building); (North Sea Protection Works); Charles Lytton/© 2011 Photos.com, a division of Getty Images. All rights reserved. (Panama Canal); Shutterstock.com, (North Sea Protection Works)

Contents

An aerial view of the Golden Gate Bridge

The Panama Canal

❋ The Panama Canal stretches from Colón to Panama City, Panama.
❋ Construction took place from 1904 to 1914.
❋ The canal is roughly fifty miles (eighty-one kilometers) long.
❋ The cost of the Panama canal was $352 million.

North Sea Protection Works

❋ The North Sea Protection Works is located in the Netherlands.
❋ They were built from 1923 to 1986.
❋ Oosterscheldedam is the longest of the works, covering 6 miles (9.7 kilometers).
❋ The cost to build was $5 billion.

The Empire State Building

❋ New York City, New York, is the home of the Empire State Building.
❋ The Empire State Building was built from 1929 to 1931.
❋ It is 1,250 feet (381 meters) in height.

The Golden Gate Bridge

❋ The Golden Gate Bridge is located in San Francisco, California, and spans a body of water known as the Golden Gate Strait.
❋ Building the Golden Gate Bridge took place from 1933 to 1937.
❋ The bridge is 8,891 feet (2,737 meters) long.
❋ The cost of building the Golden Gate Bridge was $27 million.

The Burj Khalifa

❋ The Burj Khalifa is located in Dubai, United Arab Emirates.
❋ The building gained the official title of "Tallest Building in the World" at its opening on January 4, 2010.
❋ At 2,717 feet (828 meters) tall, it is taller than any other man-made structure ever built.

The Itaipu Dam

❋ The Itaipu Dam spans the Paraná River between the Brazil and Paraguay.
❋ Construction on the dam took place from 1975 to 1991.
❋ The dam is about five miles (eight kilometers) long.
❋ It cost $18 billion to build the dam.

The Channel Tunnel

❋ The Channel Tunnel, commonly known as the Chunnel, stretches underneath the English Channel from Folkestone, England to Coquelles, France.
❋ Building the Chunnel began in 1987; it was not opened until 1994.
❋ The Chunnel is 32 miles (51.5 kilometers) long, of which 23 miles (37 kilometers) is under the sea.
❋ Completion of the tunnel cost $21 million.

CHAPTER 1

Humans Against Nature

Each of the structures in this book began as a dream to move faster, go higher, or live better. The Panama Canal, for example, was built to speed travel between the Pacific and Atlantic Oceans. Its construction required removing enough dirt and rubble to open a 16-foot-wide (5-meter) tunnel to the center of the earth.[1] The Channel Tunnel, an undersea train tunnel that stretches from Britain to France, was also built to help people travel faster. The need for speed was considered in all aspects of this project. The trains that move through the tunnel have a locomotive on each end to hasten a train's exit in case of emergency.[2]

Some structures were built to go higher than ever before. The Empire State Building, for instance, was built to fulfill a dream to construct the highest building in the world. It is so tall, there is over 17 million feet (5 million meters) of telephone wire inside it.[3] This is more than enough wire to stretch from New York City to Los Angeles, California.[4] The nearly 2,717-foot tall (828-meters) Burj Khalifa was also built to go as high as possible. The building has returned the location of Earth's tallest freestanding structure to the Middle East, where the Great Pyramid of Giza claimed this achievement for almost four millennia.[5]

This world map shows where each of the modern wonders is located.

The desire to live better is what motivated the construction of the North Sea Protection Works. These dams and barriers hold back the ocean and protect the people of the Netherlands from flooding. Its longest dam is the Oosterscheldedam. It is as long as a thousand school buses parked end to end.[6] Itaipu Dam in South America began as a vision to create electricity for the people of Paraguay and Brazil. The completed energy plant includes a dam so massive it contains enough iron and steel to build three hundred Eiffel Towers.[7]

The lights that illuminate the top of the Empire State Building change colors at various times throughout the year. In this photo, the lights are red, white, and blue to celebrate the Fourth of July holiday.

None of the structures in this book were easy to build. Each one pitted human ingenuity and perseverance against nature. In the end, human desire triumphed. Along the way, new machines were often invented and new engineering methods devised. For example, the engineers of the Golden Gate Bridge worked for months solving mathematical equations to create a bridge that could withstand 100-mile per hour (185.2-kilometer per hour) winds. Their work was done before the age of computers, with nothing more than slide rules and adding machines to crunch numbers. The result? A bridge that safely swings nearly twenty-eight feet (nine meters).[8]

As their creators imaginatively overcame obstacles, these structures became the marvels of their day. The Seven Wonders of the Modern World are examples of modern society's ability to achieve the impossible.

CHAPTER 2

The Panama Canal

The Panama Canal creates one of the longest shortcuts in the world. Before it was built, ships going from the Atlantic Ocean to the Pacific Ocean had to sail around South America. The new canal made it possible to cut through Panama, a country at the southern end of North America. This took about eight thousand miles (thirteen thousand kilometers) off the journey. It is such a useful route that thousands of cargo, military, and cruise ships travel through the canal each year.

The Need For a Canal

People had dreamed of connecting the oceans as far back as the 1500s. It would be centuries, though, before the proper machinery and know-how made a canal possible.

In the late 1800s, a canal seemed achievable. The French were the first to try. However, their machines were too small, and tropical diseases killed many workers. By the end of the century, they had given up.

The dream did not die, though. United States president Theodore Roosevelt saw how valuable a canal would be for moving goods and people. Furthermore, he was convinced a canal was essential to the defense of the United States. It would allow the American Navy's fleet of ships to move quickly from one side of the country to the other.

The Panama Canal made it possible for people to sail from the Atlantic Ocean to the Pacific Ocean without having to go around the southern tip of the South American continent.

In 1903, the United States government paid Panama $10 million for the right to build and operate a canal there.[1] The first task was to make the area safe for workers. Crews cleared brush and drained swamps, killing millions of disease-carrying mosquitoes that had devastated the French attempt.

A Cut, A Lake, and Some Locks

Soon steam shovels were digging through the hills on the Pacific side of Panama. The earth here was very loose, and landslides slowed the work. It took several years to make a cut 8 miles (13 kilometers) long. During that time, tons of earth were removed to make a channel called the Gaillard Cut.

The earth taken from the Gaillard Cut was hauled by train to the other side of the country. There it was used to make a dam across the Chagres River. Once finished, the dam backed water into a valley to create Gatun Lake.

Gatun Lake and the Gaillard Cut would form the main waters of the Panama Canal. Yet both lay above ocean waters. Therefore, ships would have to be raised and lowered to use the canal. This required structures called locks.

A lock is a giant tank used to move ships between two levels of water. A vessel moves into a lock, and the gates of the lock are closed. Water is poured into the chamber or drained out until the level inside the lock is the same as on the other side of the water that the ship is moving toward. Then the gate opens, and the ship sails out.

The locks of the Panama Canal were one of the biggest engineering challenges of the project. They were built in pairs to allow vessels to travel both ways on the canal at the same time. At 110 feet (34 meters) wide and 1,000 feet (305 meters) long, they were the largest concrete structures ever built.[2]

The steel gates for the locks were also massive. Each one weighed more than 700 tons (635 metric tons). They were opened and closed with a 40-horsepower engine.[3] This is the same size motor used to power a small boat.

A vessel coming from the Atlantic Ocean is hooked to locomotives that guide it through the Gatun Locks. These locks raise the ship 85 feet (26 meters) to Gatun Lake.

The Cost of a Canal

During the busiest construction period, almost forty-five thousand people were working on the canal. Most came from the British West Indies, but many were from the United States.

The canal was completed in 1914 at a cost of $352 million.[4] Another kind of cost was the number of deaths. Over five thousand people died from injury or illness while working to complete the canal.[5]

Through the Canal

On August 15, 1914, the first ship, the SS *Ancon*, sailed through the Panama Canal. Its journey was much the same as the trip is today.

A vessel coming from the Atlantic Ocean is hooked to locomotives that guide it through the Gatun Locks. These locks raise the ship 85 feet (26 meters) to Gatun Lake.

After a 32-mile (51-kilometer) journey across the lake, the ship sails through the Gaillard Cut. At the end of the cut, it enters the Pedro Miguel Locks. These lower the ship 30 feet (9 meters) to another lake. From here it moves through the Miraflores Locks and is let down another 52 feet (16 meters) to the Pacific Ocean. The 50-mile (80-kilometer) trip takes about eight hours. The locks by the Pacific Ocean lower ships three feet more than the Atlantic Ocean locks. This is because the sea level here is three feet lower.

The Canal Today

In 1977, the United States agreed to gradually transfer ownership of the canal to Panama. The transition was complete at the end of 1999. Since then, Panama has improved the canal by widening the Gaillard Cut and improving the locks. With these changes, the hope is that the canal will be used for many years to come.

CHAPTER 3

North Sea Protection Works

People who live in the Netherlands are fond of saying, "God created the world, but the Dutch created Holland." The Netherlands, sometimes called Holland, is a country in Europe that borders the North Sea. Its people are known as the Dutch. Much of the Netherlands lies below sea level, making it easy to flood.

For centuries, the Dutch built dikes to hold back the sea. Sometimes they built dikes around shallow water, then emptied the area using windmill-powered pumps. The water was channeled back to the ocean through man-made canals. The newly drained land, called a polder, was used to live on. Farms, towns, and even large cities have been built on polders.

Yet dikes have not always held back the sea during severe storms. When a dike broke, water often washed away houses, farms, and people. Two devastating storms—one that occurred in 1916 and another in 1953—prompted the Dutch government to build new barriers along the sea. The resulting dams and floodgates are known as the North Sea Protection Works.

The Zuiderzeeworks

In 1916, a terrible storm killed hundreds of people around the Zuider Zee, a large inlet in the northern part of the Netherlands. The government immediately planned a protection project called the Zuiderzeeworks.

The North Sea Protection Works is a series of dams and floodgates that allow the Dutch to keep water levels low so that they can build cities, towns, and farms.

First, a 19-mile-long (31-kilometer) dam was built across the Zuider Zee. The structure was made from clay, sand, stone, and "mattresses" of small trees and bushes. This dam was 25 feet (8 meters) high and as thick as a football field.[1] Some of the water inside the dam was drained, creating an area of polders that was called Flevoland. The remaining water became a freshwater lake named Ijsselmeer. This part of the North Sea Protection Works was finished in 1932.

When another huge storm blew across the North Sea in 1953, the Zuiderzeeworks held. However, nearly two thousand people in the south-western province of Zeeland were killed by flooding waters. Determined to prevent another similar disaster, the Dutch government began a program called the Delta Plan.

The Delta Plan

Zeeland is a land of peninsulas and islands interrupted by several deltas. A delta is a fan-shaped deposit of sand and soil that forms at the mouth of a river. Engineers decided that the region needed several different kinds of barriers. So they planned various structures, not sure of how the larger ones would be built. But they felt confident that as the smaller structures were constructed, the technology and expertise for making the bigger pieces would develop.[2]

First, several dikes were heightened. Then three main dams were built across the estuaries of the Rhine, Mass, and Scheldt rivers (an estuary is the place where a river meets the sea). Channels were left open for ocean vessels to get to and from Rotterdam, the Netherlands, and Antwerp, Belgium. Then it was time to build the most complex part of the project—a surge barrier that would dam the Oosterschelde estuary.

The Oosterscheldedam

The Oosterscheldedam was planned as a closed barrier. However, fishermen and conservationists knew this would destroy much of the marine life inside the dam. They persuaded the government to build a barrier that would

A quarter of the land in the Netherlands lies near or even below sea level, making it vulnerable to floods. By the thirteenth century, the Dutch were regularly using windmills to pump water off reclaimed areas that have been used for crops, settlements, and ports.

remain open most of the time, but be closed when bad weather threatened. This would minimize interference with the natural environment.

Sixty-five giant concrete piers were needed, each weighing around eighteen thousand tons (sixteen thousand metric tons) and standing as tall as a twelve-story building.[3] Two artificial islands were built in the Oosterschelde estuary for constructing the piers.

Once the piers were completed, specially made vessels towed them into the sea and strung them between the work islands and the mainland. Computers aboard the boats and on the shore guided the positioning of each. The technology was so precise, every one of the piers was placed within 4 inches (10 centimeters) of its planned position.[4] Then tons of sand and rock were piled along the bottom of the piers, anchoring them against the battering tides of the North Sea.

Next, huge steel gates were lowered between the piers. These gates could be closed by a control station on one of the work islands. The gates and mechanisms are so well engineered, the entire barrier can be closed in just one hour. The Oosterschelde storm surge barrier was finished in 1986.

Living With the Sea

The final price tag of the Delta Plan alone was $5 billion.[5] To the Dutch, the safety is well worth the money.

In addition to providing safety to the people of Holland, the dams have created new recreation areas. Roadways have been built on top of some to improve transportation routes throughout the region. Finally, the larger dams are a tourist attraction. A museum near the Oosterscheldedam describes how the dams were built.

The North Sea Protection Works has been called a wonder of the world because of its size and the technical expertise needed to create it. One professional magazine remarked, "It is unique, expensive, and quite unlike any other civil engineering project to be found on this planet."[6] It is proof that even if the Dutch did not actually create Holland, they are certainly preserving it.

CHAPTER 4

The Empire State Building

The movie audience gasped. What would King Kong do with the beautiful heroine, Fay Wray, when he got to the top of the skyscraper? Everyone watching the 1933 movie knew the gigantic ape was climbing the tallest building in the world, the Empire State Building. It was, and still is, one of the most famous structures ever built.

The Empire State Building is located in New York City, and it was the world's tallest building from 1931 until 1972. Today, only a handful of buildings rise higher.

The Race to the Sky

During the late 1800s, builders began using steel to frame tall buildings. Steel frameworks made it possible to erect taller and taller structures. Soon the skyscraper was born, and each one seemed to go higher.

Before long, some people made a competition of erecting the world's tallest building. First came the Woolworth Building in 1913. It is 792 feet (241 meters) high. The Bank of Manhattan Trust (now known as the Trump Building) topped this in 1930 at 927 feet (283 meters). The Chrysler Building was next, also in 1930. It is 1,046 feet (319 meters) tall.[1]

Yet even before the Chrysler Building was finished, investor John Jacob Raskob was making plans to go higher. He wanted to erect a building as a

The Empire State Building is the centerpiece of midtown Manhattan. People can go up to the eighty-sixth-floor observation deck and look out over the surrounding area.

tribute to America's wealth of opportunity.[2] Raskob named his dream after New York state's nickname, and the Empire State Building began taking shape.

Designing the Building

New York City zoning laws said that tall buildings could not block sunlight from reaching the street. So the 1,250-foot (381-meter) building was designed to decrease in size as it grew taller, allowing sunshine to fall to the ground.

Mail chutes, bathrooms, and elevator shafts would be built in the center of each floor, with office space around the outside. This would allow every worker to be within 25 feet (8 meters) of a window.

The building also had to include enough elevators to move thousands of people among one hundred floors. The finished structure would boast seventy-three elevators. Finally, Raskob wanted the top of his building to have a docking station for dirigibles. At the time, these airships were used for transportation.

Building the World's Tallest Structure

By March 1930, the building site had been cleared, and the footings (the parts of the base that make sure the building is not tilted to one side) were set. Then, like giant pieces from an Erector toy construction set, exactly measured beams and girders were delivered for the building's frame. These beams and girders already had rivet holes drilled into them.

As steelworkers framed the building, other workers followed behind, pouring concrete for each story's floor. Next came more workers who installed the limestone blocks and windows of the exterior walls. Behind them, electricians, plumbers, and carpenters finished the interior spaces. At the height of construction, more than three thousand people were working on the building at once.[3]

In order to keep all of these workers busy, an immense amount of supplies had to be at the right place at the right time. A company was hired for the sole purpose of organizing and delivering materials.

This "assembly line" method was new to the construction industry. It was also fast. It took only seven months for workers to get to the eighty-sixth floor. Other builders noted this efficiency and were soon utilizing the same procedures.

Obstructions

There were some problems with the construction of the Empire State Building. One was the wind. The higher in the air, the stronger the wind's force. So engineers designed special ways of connecting the framework to improve the building's strength against the wind. These and other techniques made the building so solid, it was easily repaired when an airplane accidentally crashed into it in 1945. Even so, strong winds can still cause the building to sway.

The wind also caused problems with the dirigible dock. A 200-foot (61-meter) tower on top of the eighty-sixth floor was meant to be the mooring mast for dirigibles that would help the airships dock. Two airships tested the dock, and both could barely land due to high winds. So the plan was abandoned, and an observation deck was installed at the top of the tower instead. This was the equivalent of the 102nd story.

The worst setbacks of all were the accidents. Five people were killed during construction.[4] The emphasis on constructing the building quickly may have been the cause. Yet this did not slow the pace for long. The Empire State Building was finished fourteen months after site excavation began. The grand structure alone had cost $24,718,000 to build.[5] The entire project cost about $40.9 million dollars.

Finished

The Empire State Building opened with a ceremony that involved President Herbert Hoover. On May 1, 1931, he pressed a symbolic button in the White House to turn on its lights.

A view from the Observation Deck on the 86th floor of the Empire State Building

Today, the building is filled with over ten thousand places of business, ranging from banks and offices to restaurants and jewelry stores. However there are no offices in the building's tower for safety reasons.

In addition, millions of tourists visit the eighty-sixth-floor observation deck each year. The 102nd-floor tower observation deck has been closed to the public, because officials determined it was not safe.

Raskob succeeded in building a tribute to his beloved country. The result was so spectacular, in fact, that even though the Empire State Building is no longer the tallest building in the world, it has become a symbol of America known around the globe.

CHAPTER 5

The Golden Gate Bridge

Few people visit San Francisco, California, without seeing the Golden Gate Bridge. This splendid, bright orange structure spans the entrance to San Francisco Bay, connecting the city to northern California. The Golden Gate Bridge is 8,981 feet (2,737 meters) long.[1] It was the longest suspension bridge in the world for twenty-seven years after it was completed in 1937.

We Need a Bridge

San Francisco sits at the end of a peninsula, separated from northern California by the Golden Gate Strait. A strait is a narrow body of water that joins two larger bodies of water. For many years the only way to cross the strait was by ferry.

During the 1920s, the ferries became more and more crowded, and people often waited for hours, and even days to cross. A bridge seemed like a logical solution, and a group began raising money for the project.

Other people thought the idea was foolish. They believed that the constant fog, high winds, earthquake problems, and strong ocean currents made a bridge impossible. They called it the "bridge that couldn't be built."[2]

The Golden Gate Bridge connects the city of San Francisco to Marin County, California. The bridge's orange paint, called International Orange, make it very recognizable.

Strauss's Certainty

Engineer Joseph Baerman Strauss disagreed. He designed a suspension bridge he felt could withstand all of these natural forces. His bridge would consist of two towers strung with thick metal cables that held up a six-lane road. It would need the tallest towers, the largest piers, and the longest and thickest cables ever built. Strauss was confident it could be done.[3]

Work on the Bridge Begins

Work on the bridge began in January 1933 when enormous concrete blocks were laid on either side of the strait and fastened to bedrock. The bridge's cables would be attached to beams and cemented into the blocks. These anchors would keep the weight of the bridge from bending the towers toward each other.

Meanwhile, concrete piers were being built to hold each tower. Strauss and other engineers designed the bridge so the two towers could be as close together as possible while still creating the needed span of 4,200 feet (1,280 meters). Therefore, the position of each pier was determined by engineering considerations rather than by the convenience of any particular site. This created problems.

The northern pier was situated in shallow water, and it went up easily. But the southern pier had to be built in deep ocean water. A special kind of dam had to be built before the pier could be constructed. This held ocean waters back so that workers could complete construction of the pier. The San Francisco pier was finally finished in late 1935.

The Towers

Now the towers could be erected on the top of each pier. A crane hoisted land-built sections into place, then workers fastened them together. The finished towers stood 746 feet (227 meters) tall.

Suspension cables were then strung from the anchor on one side of the bridge, over the towers, and into the anchor on the other side. Each one was about 36 inches (91 centimeters) in diameter. The two cables contained 80,000 miles (128,720 kilometers) of steel wire, enough to circle the earth three times.[4]

The exact sag of the cables was carefully calculated. The cables had to be tight enough to support the road below the bridge. They also had to be loose enough to allow the bridge to move due to stress or temperature changes. This flexibility would keep the structure from cracking during earthquakes, storms, or extreme weather changes.

Next, the cables for the road were hung from the suspension cables. They were each positioned to make the road 220 feet (67 meters) above the water so that United States Navy ships could pass under the bridge.

Building the Road

The road (U.S. Highway 101) was built in sections, starting at each of the towers and moving out in both directions at the same pace. This kept the strain on the towers and cables even. Sadly, ten men were killed while building the road. This brought the total number of deaths during the bridge's construction to eleven.[5]

Finally, it was time to pave the roadway deck and paint the bridge its unique International Orange color. The bridge was finished in 1937, four years after it was begun. It had cost a total of $27 million.[6]

Success

On May 27, 1937, two hundred thousand people celebrated the opening of the Golden Gate Bridge by walking across it. The next day an official dedication ceremony was held, and the day after that, the bridge was opened to traffic.

Since then the "bridge that couldn't be built" has been used by millions of people. It has been closed due to bad weather only three times, and it survived a large earthquake in 1989. Today, engineers are working to make it even more earthquake-proof, ensuring that the Golden Gate Bridge will remain a San Francisco icon for years to come.

CHAPTER 6

The Burj Khalifa

It's not hard to pick out Burj Khalifa. It is the building that soars above Dubai's highest skyscrapers, making them look like toys beneath it. Yet Burj Khalifa is not just the tallest building in Dubai. At 2,717 feet (828 meters), Burj Khalifa is the tallest building in the world.[1]

Dubai is a city in an emirate also named Dubai. An emirate is like a state or a province. Dubai Emirate is part of the United Arab Emirates, a small country on the Persian Gulf.

The city of Dubai grew quickly during the 1990s to become a financial center and popular tourist destination. It soon became known for its over-the-top structures. This desert city boasts an indoor ski hill and a luxurious hotel built to resemble a sail. It is also home to a housing development of man made islands shaped like a map of the world. Therefore, it was no surprise when ground was broken there in 2004 to build the tallest building on the globe.

Burj Khalifa opened in 2010. The 160-story skyscraper, topped with a 700-foot (213-meters) steel spire, is more than 1,000 feet (305 meters) higher than the previous record holder, the Taipei 101 in Taiwan.[2]

A Flower Made of Steel

The hymenocallis, a flower with spiraling petals, inspired Burj Khalifa's design. Three wings in the shape of a Y extend from a central core. These

The Burj Khalifa stands tall over the city of Dubai in the United Arab Emirates.

wings rise skyward in large sections. Each section is set back from the one below it, and the sections on each wing vary in height.

The staggering creates a spiraling effect. The spiraling design increases the number of views from the building to the Persian Gulf. It also allows lots of sunlight into the building. A façade of aluminum, stainless steel, and glass make the building shimmer in the desert sun.

A Vertical City

Burj Khalifa can hold 35,000 people.[3] It is sometimes called a vertical city because it contains many of the things found in a normal city. There are apartments, business offices, hotel rooms, fitness centers, restaurants, grocery markets, a day care, and even a mall. The highest swimming pool in the world is on the 123rd floor. The highest house of worship is the mosque on the 158th floor.

A number of floors are dedicated to making the building run. Some are electrical sub-stations; others are filled with water tanks and pumps. A few floors are devoted to communication equipment for broadcasting.

Burj Khalifa's 124th floor is an observation area. Its walls are made of glass. The area has a terrace for outdoor viewing, making it one of the world's highest outdoor observation decks. On a clear day it's possible to see 60 miles (97 km) into the distance and across the Persian Gulf to Iran.[4, 5]

Planning the Building

Building the world's tallest skyscraper presented several design challenges. First of all, the building needed to be safe in the case of a fire. So engineers had all of the stairwells surrounded in concrete.

Another challenge was figuring out how to move people up and down inside the building. Because an elevator is not able to travel 160 stories, there had to be a system of elevators that would work like vertical roads. Some elevators function as shuttles. They travel several stories before stopping to let people unload and board elevators that move floor by floor.

One of the biggest design challenges was the wind. Winds at high elevations are powerful, so engineers must find ways to make tall buildings especially sturdy. The designers of Burj Khalifa used a wind tunnel to test their ideas. They found that their Y-shaped base and staggered levels would help the soaring skyscraper withstand the wind[6] Engineers also made the building slightly flexible so it could sway in the wind rather than break. This sway is so small it cannot be felt.

Going Up

Construction on Burj Khalifa began in January 2004 with the sinking of almost 200 column-shaped foundations known as pilings. Each piling was buried more than 164 feet (50 meters) deep to create a sturdy anchor.

The Burj Khalifa defines the Dubai skyline.

It took more than four years for workers to build up to and complete the 160th floor. Next came the erection of the spire. Finally, the outside of Burj Khalifa was clad. As finishing touches were put on the building, the landscaping around it was also completed. Acres of park filled with flowers, trees, pools, and water fountains surround the building.

People Power

It took about 12,000 people to build Burj Khalifa.[7] Among them were engineers, architects, electricians, plumbers, drafters, interior decorators, mechanics, carpenters, and thousands of construction workers.

Many of the construction workers were immigrants from South Asia who were not always treated well. In a place where the average monthly income was around $2,000, these workers earned under $200 a month.[8] Many lived in labor camps where they shared a small room with several other laborers.[9] Furthermore, the workers were often exposed to dangerous situations.[10] In spite of these poor working conditions, Burj Khalifa was completed in late 2009.

On January 4, 2010, Dubai officials held a huge ceremony to celebrate its opening. Fireworks and a dazzling light show lit up the sky, while the water fountains around the skyscraper were programmed to dance to traditional and modern music.

Wave of the Future?

It cost about one and a half billion dollars to build Burj Khalifa.[11] Many people have criticized the use of so much money and resources to build the skyscraper. They believe it was nothing more than an opportunity for Dubai to boast about another spectacular building.[12] Others have said that tall buildings are the wave of the future.[13] Indeed, there are already plans underway in other countries to build even taller skyscrapers. Yet no matter how they feel about the Burj Khalifa itself, few people would deny it is an incredible engineering feat.

CHAPTER 7

The Itaipu Dam

It is hard to imagine a hydroelectric dam large enough to supply all the electric power needed to energize an entire country. Yet that is exactly what Itaipu Dam does. Located in South America between Brazil and Paraguay, the Itaipu Dam supplies nearly all of Paraguay's electricity and about one fourth of Brazil's.[1] It is, in fact, the largest renewable power plant in the world.[2]

A Cooperative Effort

In 1973, Brazil and Paraguay decided to work together to build a hydroelectric dam on the Paraná River. The Paraná, the seventh largest river in the world, runs for several miles along the border that these two countries share. The dam site was chosen at a place called Itaipu.

In 1975, earth-moving machines were used to dig a channel that would change the course of the river. This exposed the riverbed so the dam could be constructed. Diverting the river involved moving millions of tons of earth and rock and took almost three years.

Once the space was ready, five different dams were built. The main dam was in the center. It was as high as a sixty-five-story building.[3] Two buttress dams were built on either side of it, and each of these was flanked by an embankment dam. Together, the structure was about five miles

The Itaipu Dam was built on the Paraná River, bordering the nations of Brazil and Paraguay.

(eight kilometers) long.[4] When the five dams were completed in October 1982, the diversion channel was blocked, and water began rising behind the dam. Then, crews went out in boats to collect animals endangered by the rising water.[5]

Eventually, the released river created a reservoir over 14,000 square miles (36,260 square kilometers) in size. This is larger than the combined size of Massachusetts and Connecticut.

The Powerhouse

In an effort to stop water from the Paraná from flowing over the dam, eighteen enormous concrete pipes called penstocks were lined up vertically against the 5-mile (8-kilometer) dam. At the bottom of each penstock was a turbine and a generator. These eighteen generators formed the powerhouse that would create the electricity.

Each penstock would channel water from the reservoir to the power-house. The flowing water would spin the turbines, driving the generators to create electricity.

The first generators were ready to begin work in May 1984. Two or three more went into operation each year after that. By March 1991, the last generator was up and running.

Delivering Electricity

As the dam and powerhouse were being built, a system of transmission lines was constructed from Itaipu to cities in Paraguay and Brazil. These would create a power grid to carry the electricity from the plant to the people.

The many components of the dam called for a massive labor force. At the height of construction, thirty thousand people were working on the project. The total cost of Itaipu was $18 billion.[6]

A close-up view of the Itaipu Dam turbine water intake pipes. The Itaipu Dam's eighteen turbines produce 12,600 megawatts of electricity, making it the largest hydroelectric power plant in the world.

Itaipu's Success

The Itaipu Dam has been an overwhelming success. Its energy production has broken records, and in 2000 the dam produced a record 93.4 million megawatt-hours of energy.[7] This is enough to supply all of California.[8] Plus, Itaipu emits no pollutants.

Itaipu was an immense engineering feat. It is said that if the technical drawings for the project were stacked up, they would rise to the height of a fifty-story building.[9] Perhaps even more significant, though, is Itaipu's testament to how cooperation between nations can benefit all.

CHAPTER 8

The Channel Tunnel

Traveling in a train under the floor of the sea seems like something from a science fiction movie. Yet the Channel Tunnel is a reality. It connects France to England and is often referred to as the Chunnel.

An Easier Way to Travel

Britain is separated from Europe's mainland by a strip of water called the English Channel. For centuries, the only way to cross the channel was by boat or airplane. Both were time-consuming and often uncomfortable.

Several solutions had been proposed over the years, including a tunnel, a bridge, and a combination of both. But the expertise for any project was not available until the 1980s. Then, engineers believed a tunnel through the soft rock at the bottom of the channel was possible.

Designing the Channel Tunnel

Knowing that an automobile tunnel would present too many ventilation problems, engineers proposed a tunnel for trains that could carry motor vehicles. These trains would be 14 feet (4 meters) across—the widest ever built.[1]

Entrance to the Channel Tunnel, or Chunnel

The resulting design was of three tunnels that ran parallel to each other. One was for trains going from Britain to France and another for trains moving from France to Britain. The third tunnel was for maintenance and emergency vehicles. It would run between the two.

Sonar and borings helped engineers determine the best route for the tunnel. It would cross the channel at one of its narrowest places, the Strait of Dover. The tunnel would begin at Folkestone, England. There it would dive underground for 32 miles (51.5 kilometers) to emerge at Coquelles, France. Twenty-three miles (37 kilometers) of the tunnel would run 150 feet (46 meters) under the bed of the sea.[2]

Tunneling Through the Earth

Building began in 1987 when shafts were dug into the earth on each side of the channel. Then specially designed tunnel boring machines (TBMs) were lowered into the shafts. Each TBM was as long as two football fields.[3] Their cutting heads were 30 feet (9 meters) in diameter.

As each machine cut its way through rock, one driver and a computerized laser guidance system kept it on course. The resulting debris was moved out by a conveyor belt, then taken back to the appropriate shaft.

On the British side of the channel, the material was dumped into an artificial lagoon created by a huge seawall. The water eventually evaporated, and a new piece of England was created. On the French side of the channel, the debris was dumped into a lake near the coast. Once filled, it was planted with grass.

As each TBM moved forward, machinery at the back lined the tunnel walls with pieces of pre-shaped concrete. These were later reinforced to make each tunnel wall 5 feet (2 meters) thick.[4]

When the tunnels were 300 feet (91 meters) apart, the TBMs were stopped. The remaining distance between the tunnels would be drilled with smaller machines so that the two ends could be perfectly aligned. Then the two tunnels would become one.

The TBMs had no reverse gear, and they could not be backed out of the tunnels. So when their job was finished, the machines on the English side were aimed downward and each burrowed itself into the bottom of the sea. The machines were dismantled except for the cutting heads, which were too difficult and expensive to remove. Instead, the cutting heads were left in the seabed and the holes were filled with concrete. Once the tunnels were joined, the French TBMs drove through the English side, where they were pulled out of the shaft.

Tracks, Pipes, and Wires

Next, workers laid the railroad tracks. Then came the piping and pumping equipment that would carry cold water through the tunnel. The cold water is needed to cool down the heat caused by the friction of the trains.

Electricians wired security systems, signaling, and lighting. Workers built crossover tracks between the two tunnels. This way trains could continue running even when one of the tunnels had to be shut down.

The Channel Tunnel was finished at the end of 1993. On May 6, 1994, it opened with a ceremony attended by Queen Elizabeth II of Britain and French President François Mitterrand. Cost estimates vary for the project. The highest is $21 billion, making the Chunnel the most expensive civil engineering project in history.[5]

The Chunnel in the Twenty-First Century

Since opening, the Channel Tunnel has become a popular way to travel. People drive their cars onto a train at one end of the tunnel, then sit in the car while the train carries them to the other side. Moving at 100 miles per hour (161 kilometers per hour), this takes only thirty-five minutes, replacing a ninety-minute ferry ride.

Eurotrain entering Channel Tunnel on the French side for a test run in October, 2010

Furthermore, some trains offer passenger service from London to Paris or Brussels. This takes about three hours. A high-speed rail link on the English side is currently being extended all the way to London.

In its first five years of operation, 28 million passengers and 12 million tons (10.9 metric tons) of freight moved through the Channel Tunnel.[6] To many Europeans and tourists, it is a fantastic new transportation system. To engineers, it is a marvel.

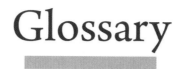

Glossary

bedrock—The solid rock that lies beneath loose material such as soil.

boring machine—A machine that is used to dig cylinder-shaped tunnels in the ground.

canal—A long and narrow man-made waterway meant for boats to pass through or to provide water used for irrigation.

channel—A deep, narrow body of water separating two close land-masses.

delta—A fan-shaped deposit of sand and soil that forms at the mouth of a river.

dirigible—An airship such as a blimp.

estuary—The region at the mouth of a river where the river's fresh-water mixes with the saltwater from a sea.

ferry—A small vessel that moves people or vehicles across a body of water and departs and returns on a consistent schedule.

girder—A horizontal support beam that supports vertical beams used to construct a building.

hydroelectricity—Electricity created by water-powered turbine generators.

inlet—A narrow passage of water leading to a bay or lagoon.

straight—A narrow body of water that joins two larger bodies of water.

turbine—A machine containing rotating blades that are turned by flowing water.

ventilation—The process of circulating air so that contaminated air is replaced with fresh air.

Chapter Notes

Chapter 1. Humans Against Nature

1. American Society of Civil Engineers, "Seven Wonders of the Modern World," 1996–2004, <http://www.asce.org/history/seven_wonders.cfm#neder> (November 4, 2004).

2. Cathy Newman, "The Light at the End of the Chunnel," *National Geographic,* May 1994, p. 44.

3. "The Empire State Building," *WonderClub.com,* n.d., <http://wonderclub.com/WorldWonders/EmpireHistory.html> (October 18, 2004).

4. "Empire State Building Trivia and Cool Facts," *20th Century History,* n.d., <http://history1900s.about.com/library/misc/blempirefacts.htm> (October 18, 2004).

5. "Burj Khalifa—The Tower," <http://www.burjkhalifa.ae/language/en-us/the-tower.aspx> (August 24, 2012).

6. "Oosterschelde," *4Reference,* n.d., <http://www.4reference.net/encyclopedias/wikipedia/Oosterschelde.html> (October 18, 2004).

7. American Society of Civil Engineers, "Seven Wonders of the Modern World."

8. Golden Gate Bridge: Research Library, "Bridge Design and Construction Statistics," 2004, <http://www.goldengatebridge.org/research/factsGGBDesign.html?version=test#Bridgestats> (November 3, 2004).

Chapter 2. The Panama Canal

1. Panama Canal History, "American Canal Construction," 2001, <http://www.pancanal.com/eng/history/history/american.html> (November 4, 2004).

2. Neil Parkyn, ed., *The Seventy Wonders of the Modern World* (London: Thames and Hudson Ltd, 2002), p. 262.

3. Bob Cullen, "A Man, A Plan, A Canal: Panama Rises," *Smithsonian,* March 2004, p. 47.

4. Panama Canal History Museum, "canalmuseum.com," 2002, <http://www.canalmuseum.com/> (November 4, 2004).

5. Cullen, p. 47.

Chapter 3. North Sea Protection Works

1. National Geographic Society, as reprinted by *WonderClub.com*, "The North Sea Protection Works," n.d., <http://wonderclub.com/WorldWonders/ProtectionHistory.html> (November 4, 2004).

2. Kees d'Angremond, "From Disaster to Delta Project: The Storm Flood of 1953," *Terra et Aqua*, March 2003, <http://www.iadc-dredging.com/downloads/terra/terra-et-aqua_nr90_01.pdf> (November 4, 2004).

3. Larry Kohl, "The Oosterschelde Barrier: Man Against the Sea," *National Geographic*, October 1986, p. 532.

4. Ibid., p. 534.

5. Ibid., p. 527.

6. National Geographic Society, as reprinted at *WonderClub.com*, "The North Sea Protection Works."

Chapter 4. The Empire State Building

1. "Landmarks in American Civil Engineering History: Empire State Building," *Civil Engineering*, November/December 2002, p. 125.

2. Jeff Glasser, "Race to the Sky," *U.S. News and World Report*, June 30, 2003, p. 50.

3. Ibid., p. 53.

4. The History Net: 20th Century History, "Empire State Building Trivia and Cool Facts," 2004, <http://history1900s.about.com/library/misc/blempirefacts.htm> (November 3, 2004).

5. Ibid., p. 1.

Chapter 5. The Golden Gate Bridge

1. Golden Gate Bridge: Research Library, "Bridge Design and Construction Statistics," 2004, <http://www.goldengatebridge.org/research/factsGGBDesign.html?version=test#Bridgestats> (November 3, 2004).

2. John Bernard McGloin, "Symphonies in Steel: Bay Bridge and the Golden Gate," *Museum of the City of San Francisco*, n.d., <http://www.sfmuseum.net/hist9/mcgloin.html> (November 4, 2004).

3. Ibid., p. 4.

4. Golden Gate Bridge: Research Library, "Bridge Design and Construction Statistics."

5. Golden Gate Bridge: Research Library, "Frequently Asked Questions About the Golden Gate Bridge," 2004, <http://www.goldengatebridge.org/ research/facts.html> (November 4, 2004).

6. Neil Parkyn, ed., *The Seventy Wonders of the Modern World* (London: Thames and Hudson Ltd., 2002), p. 235.

Chapter 6. The Burj Khalifa

1. Kamin, Blair. "Burj Khalifa, Dubai." *Architectural Record* 198.8 (2010): 78.

2. Ibid.

3. Melvin, Jeremy. "On A Clear Day, You Can See Iran From the Burj Khalifa." *Architectural Review* 227.1356 (2010): 019-020.

4. Thomas, Jr. Landon. "Dubai Opens A Tower To Beat All." *New York Times* (January 4, 2010). http://www.nytimes.com/2010/01/05/business/global/05tower.html

5. Melvin.

6. Belleza, Irish Eden. "Burj Khalifa: Towering Challenge For Builders." *Gulf News* (January 4, 2010). http://gulfnews.com/business/property/burj-khalifa-towering-challenge-for-builders-1.561802

7. Burj Khalifa, "The Tower." http://www.burjkhalifa.ae/language/en-us/the-tower/construction.aspx

8. "Building Towers, Cheating Workers: Exploitation of Migrant Construction Workers in the United Arab Emirates." *Human Rights Watch* (November 2006) Volume 18 No. 8(E), p. 7.

9. Ibid., p. 23.

10. Ibid., p. 10.

11. Kamin.

12. Ibid.

13. Ibid.

Chapter 7. The Itaipu Dam

1. Itaipu Binancional—The World's Largest Power Plant, "Production," n.d., <http://www.itaipu.gov.br/english/dados/produ.htm> (November 4, 2004).

2. Itaipu Binancional—The World's Largest Power Plant, "Historical Background," n.d., <http://www.itaipu.gov.br/english/empre/histo.htm> (November 4, 2004).

3. American Society of Civil Engineers, "Seven Wonders of the Modern World," 1996–2004, <http://www.asce.org/history/seven_wonders.cfm#neder> (November 4, 2004).

4. Neil Parkyn, ed., *The Seventy Wonders of the Modern World* (London: Thames and Hudson Ltd., 2002), p. 267.

5. Ibid., p. 269.

6. Ibid., p. 267.

7. Itaipu Binancional—The World's Largest Power Plant, "Production."

8. Gregory T. Pope, "The Seven Wonders of the Modern World," *Popular Mechanics,* December 1995, p. 50.

9. "The Powerhouse," *The Geographical Magazine,* April 1996, p. 13.

Chapter 8. The Channel Tunnel

1. Gregory T. Pope, "The Seven Wonders of the Modern World," *Popular Mechanics,* December 1995, p. 52.

2. Neil Parkyn, ed., *The Seventy Wonders of the Modern World* (London: Thames and Hudson Ltd., 2002), p. 242.

3. Cathy Newman, "The Light at the End of the Chunnel," *National Geographic,* May 1994, p. 40.

4. Pope, p. 52.

5. PBS Online, "Channel Tunnel," *Building Big: Wonders of the World Data Bank,* 2000–2001, <http://www.pbs.org/wgbh/buildingbig/wonder/structure/channel.html> (November 4, 2004).

6. Ibid., p. 2.

Further Reading
and Internet Addresses

Further Reading

Ash, Russell. *Great Wonders of the World.* New York: Dorling Kindersley, Inc., 2006.

Graham, Ian. *Tremendous Tunnels.* Mankato, Minn.: Amicus, 2011.

Lynette, Rachel. *The Panama Canal.* San Diego, Calif.: KidHaven Press, 2005.

Riggs, Kate. *Golden Gate Bridge.* Mankato, Minn.: Creative Education, 2009.

Steele, Philip. *Wonders of the World.* New York: Kingfisher, 2007.

Weil, Ann. *The World's Most Amazing Dams.* Chicago, Ill.: Raintree, 2012.

Internet Addresses

Golden Gate Bridge: American Experience— WGBH | PBS
   <http://www.pbs.org/wgbh/americanexperience/films/goldengate/>

Seven Wonders—American Society of Civil Engineers
   <www.asce.org/Content.aspx?id=2147487305>

Index